Off to Work!

Eric Christopher Meyer

Contents

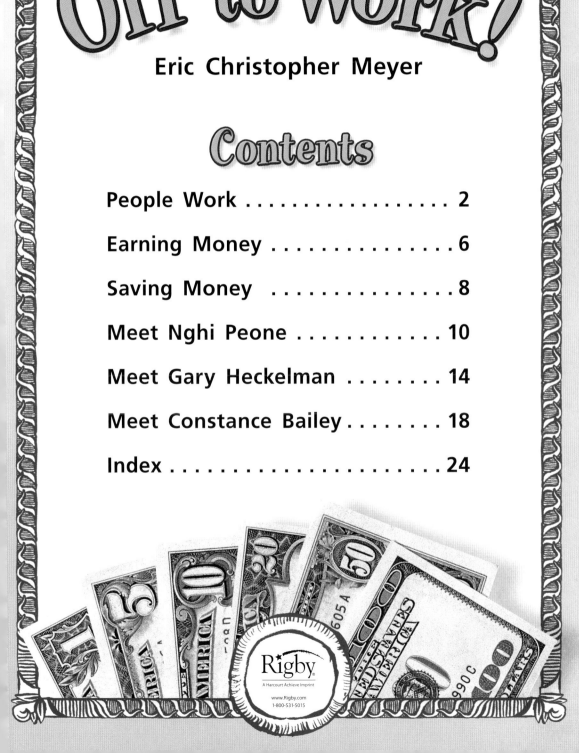

Rigby
A Harcourt Achieve Imprint
www.Rigby.com
1-800-531-5015

People Work

What kind of work will you do when you grow up?

People work at all kinds of jobs. Some people work by making goods. A car is a kind of good.

Many goods are very important. Some people make medicines to keep you healthy.

Sometimes people work in businesses that help other people. Work done to help others is called a service.

Firefighters, doctors, and police officers have kinds of service jobs. They help people in their communities.

Earning Money

People earn money at their jobs. Money lets them pay for things they need and things they want.

People pay for their homes.

Food at restaurants costs money.

Money pays for fun, too.

Saving Money

Saving money is important, too. Here's what might happen if you save your money.

You work to earn money.	→	You start saving your money.	→	You put your savings in the bank.

You add more money that you earn.

You have enough to buy a new bike!

Meet Nghi Peone

Nghi (NEE) Peone was born in Vietnam in 1962. She came to the United States when she was sixteen.

Nghi works at Ann Marie's Café.

Nghi spends some of the money she earns on food for her family.

Nghi does many things at her job.

She prepares sack lunches.

She brings food to people.

She collects money.

Nghi gets paid.

Meet Gary Heckelman

Gary Heckelman was born in New York in 1959. He has loved books his whole life.

Gary owns and works at Raising Children Bookstore.

Gary spends some of the money he earns on clothes.

Gary does many things at his job.

He orders new books.

He unpacks boxes of new books.

He helps his customers.

Gary gets paid.

Meet Constance Bailey

Constance Bailey was born in California in 1951. She likes to bake cookies and cakes.

Constance owns and works at a bakery called the Hudson Valley Dessert Company.

Constance spends some of the money she earns on her home.

Constance does many things at her job.

She takes phone orders.

She makes pastries.

She keeps the store clean.

Constance gets paid.

Here are some important events in the lives of Nghi, Gary, and Constance.

When were you born on this timeline?

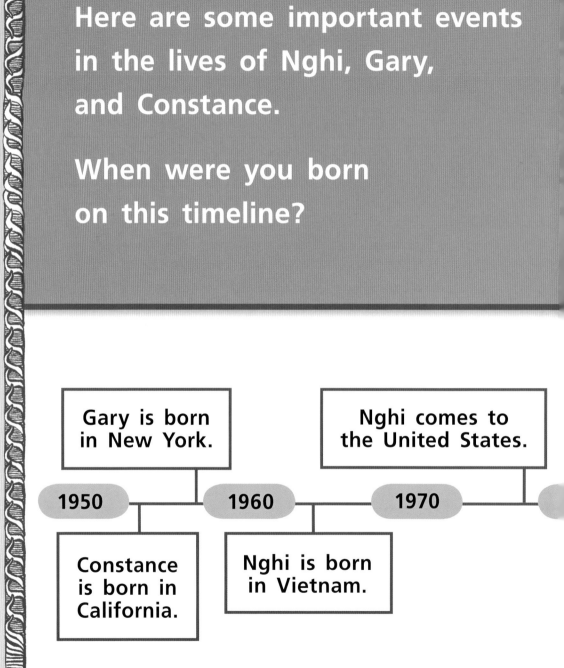

Gary is born in New York.

Nghi comes to the United States.

1950   1960   1970

Constance is born in California.

Nghi is born in Vietnam.

Nghi

Gary

Constance

Constance opens
her bakery.

1990 — 2000 — 2010

Gary opens
his bookstore.

Nghi begins
work at Ann
Marie's.

Index